CW00506384

GCSE 9–1
MACBETH
BY WILLIAM SHAKESPEARE
GREAT ANSWERS

SCHOLASTIC

Published in the UK by Scholastic, 2020

Scholastic Distribution Centre, Bosworth Avenue,
Tournament Fields, Warwick, CV34 6UQ

Scholastic Education, Scholastic Ireland, 89E Lagan Road,
Dublin Industrial Estate, Glasnevin, Dublin, D11 HP5F

© Scholastic Limited, 2020

**A CIP catalogue record for this book is available from the
British Library.**

ISBN 978-1407-18397-8

Printed in India
Paper made from wood grown in sustainable forests and other
controlled sources.

2 3 4 5 6 7 8 9   2 3 4 5 6 7 8 9 0 1

Authors
Richard Durant and Cindy Torn

Editorial team
Audrey Stokes, Vicki Yates, Kate Pedlar, Julia Roberts

Typesetting
Jayne Rawlings/Oxford Raw Design

Design team
Dipa Mistry

Contents

About this book

This book is designed to demonstrate what a great answer for your AQA GCSE English Literature exam question on *Macbeth* (Paper 1, Section A) looks like. It demonstrates a step-by-step process from first sight of the question through to a full answer. This process shows you how to approach each step, from analysing what the question is asking you to do, to planning your answer, showing how it meets the assessment objectives for the exam paper and finally presenting a great answer and an examiner's response. All the answers in this book have been written in the light of advice from examiners and using tips drawn from the examiners' reports over the last few years.

It is important to note that one question can give rise to multiple different great answers. What these great answers all have in common is that they are based on an excellent interpretation with sound exploration of evidence. Great answers are not *right* answers, they are rich and well-argued answers.

In this book you will find the following features that will help you understand how to achieve that all-important great answer in your exam.

Zoom in on the question

Starting with this moment in the play, explore how Shakespeare presents the relationship between Macbeth and the supernatural.

Write about:

- how Shakespeare presents the relationship between Macbeth and the supernatural in this extract
- how Shakespeare presents the relationship between Macbeth and the supernatural in the play as a whole.

First, focus on the extract to 'anchor' the answer and to explore some details. (AO1/AO2)

Concentrate on Shakespeare's ideas and how he chooses his words to present those ideas. (AO1/AO2)

Analysis of the question to help you focus on what the question is actually asking you.

Start with the extract but explain details with references to other parts of the play. (AO3)

Stay relevant to the question focus: how Macbeth both resists and uses the supernatural. (AO1)

AO1 The witches and Macbeth try to use each other. Is he a victim of evil? Do evil forces control and corrupt him? Note how Shakespeare shows us who has the upper hand at times during the play.

AO2 Note the strength of Macbeth's words (which suggest violence and scorn) here and elsewhere. He changes through the play, as do audience reactions to him. Compare the witches' sarcasm and trickery with Macbeth's own scorn ('Filthy hags!').

AO3 Consider significance of differences between contemporary and modern beliefs about evil and the supernatural.

Ideas to help you cover the AOs for each question and matching colour-coded commentary within the answers to show you how these are achieved.

The play very intensely focuses on the Macbeths, their thoughts, feelings and plans. As a result it is difficult for the audience to understand what sort of ruler Macbeth is, how he is viewed by his people and by England, and how much time is passing. Shakespeare uses the Lords to summarise these broader aspects of the action so that he can maintain claustrophobic attention on the Macbeths [6] and their crimes and obsessions. In the extract, for example, we learn the important information that neither Fleance nor Macduff have been captured and that this is a threat to Macbeth.[7] Other Lords give us important information at other times in the play;[8] for example, near the end, Angus reports that there are 'revolts' (rebellions) against Macbeth in Scotland (which will make his defeat easier), and of course Shakespeare avoids the need for a battle scene on-stage at the start of the play by having Ross (and the captain) summarise the battle for us.

[6] **AO2:** insight into Shakespeare's craft as a dramatist.

[7] **AO1:** precise choice of indirect references to illustrate points.

[8] **AO3:** comparison of use of techniques in the extract and in the play as a whole.

Paragraph	Content		Timing
1	Intro – use the question prep to establish focus of answer, and my key angle: Macbeth's heroism.		9.40
2	Explore extract – evidence of heroic bravery/approval.		9.47
3	Other early evidence of Macbeth's bravery and heroism. Focus on AO2 language.	Refer back to extract and question focus throughout. Question what Shakespeare might be implying about Macbeth's character.	10.02
4	How Macbeth is presented in Act 5 (including how manliness interacts with bravery and heroism).		10.13
5	Conclusion – is Macbeth a brave hero or a cowardly villain?		10.22

Essay plans and timings to help you plan more efficiently.

DO IT!

Now use what you've learned to answer the following AQA exam-style question.

Read the extract from Act 3 Scene 6 of *Macbeth* on page 22.

Starting with this speech, write about how Shakespeare explores suspicion in *Macbeth*.

Write about:

- what Lennox hints about suspicion in this speech
- how Shakespeare Lennox hints about suspicion in this speech.

[30 marks]
AO4 [4 marks]

AQA exam-style questions using the *same* extract provided for the Great Answer analysis which precedes it.

Exam-style questions using previously unseen text extracts, allowing you to put into practice the skills you've learned and create a great answer by yourself.

Online answers

Designed to guide you towards structuring a really 'great answer' and consolidate your understanding through thought and application (including an AO breakdown). Remember: it is important to write your own answers before checking online at **www.scholastic.co.uk/gcse**.

Advice for students

✓ **Know your text well.** This will help you to demonstrate your knowledge and understanding in the exam. Concentrate on knowing the text well rather than predicting questions.

✓ **Read the question carefully and answer the question.** Be sure you are answering the question you have chosen and *not* the one that you would have preferred to see on the paper.

✓ **Take time to think about and plan your answer.** Gathering your thoughts will give you space to address the question and choose appropriate references and details to support and develop your answer.

✓ **Demonstrate your knowledge by referencing parts of the play.** But make sure it is relevant, you don't get extra marks for more quotations, but you do get more marks for making interesting comments about the references you have selected.

✓ **Read the extracts very carefully.** It is helpful to place the extract in the context of the play – at what point, what happened before and/or after, which characters are involved, how does it link to other parts of the text. Be sure that you understand the meaning and context of quotations you choose from the extract.

✓ **Recognise that 'writer's methods' means anything the writer has done deliberately.** This covers the writer's use of language and techniques, the structure of the text and characterisation.

✓ **Understand the connection between the writer's methods and the writer's ideas.** It might be helpful to think about *how* the writer does something and *why* the writer does something.

✓ **Link comments on contextual factors/ideas to the text.** Keep in mind that context informs but should never dominate your reading of the text; the text comes first. Relating the extract to the whole text is a valid approach to context.

Read the following **extract** from Act 4 Scene 1 of *Macbeth* and then answer the question that follows.

At this point in the play, Macbeth has just asked the witches if Banquo's children will ever be kings of Scotland.

ALL THE WITCHES
Show his eyes, and grieve his heart;
Come like shadows, so depart!

A show of EIGHT KINGS, *the last with a glass in his hand;*
BANQUO'S GHOST *following.*

MACBETH
Thou art too like the spirit of Banquo. Down!
Thy crown does sear mine eyeballs. And thy hair,
5   Thou other gold-bound brow, is like the first.
A third, is like the former. Filthy hags!
Why do you show me this? A fourth! Start, eyes!
What, will the line stretch out to the crack of doom?
Another yet! A seventh! I'll see no more!
10   And yet the eighth appears, who bears a glass
Which shows me many more; and some I see
That twofold balls and treble sceptres carry.
Horrible sight! Now I see 'tis true;
For the blood-bolter'd Banquo smiles upon me,
15   And points at them for his. What, is this so?

FIRST WITCH
Ay, sir, all this is so. But why
Stands Macbeth thus amazedly?
Come, sisters, cheer we up his sprites,
And show the best of our delights.
20   I'll charm the air to give a sound,
While you perform your antic round,
That this great King may kindly say,
Our duties did his welcome pay.

Music. The WITCHES *dance and then vanish with* HECATE.

Starting with this moment in the play, explore how Shakespeare presents the relationship between Macbeth and the supernatural.

Write about:

- how Shakespeare presents the relationship between Macbeth and the supernatural in this extract

- how Shakespeare presents the relationship between Macbeth and the supernatural in the play as a whole.

[30 marks]
AO4 [4 marks]

Zoom in on the question

Starting with this moment in the play, explore how Shakespeare presents the relationship between Macbeth and the supernatural.

First, focus on the extract to 'anchor' the answer and to explore some details. (AO1/AO2)

Write about:

- how Shakespeare presents the relationship between Macbeth and the supernatural in this extract

- how Shakespeare presents the relationship between Macbeth and the supernatural in the play as a whole.

Concentrate on Shakespeare's ideas and how he chooses his words to present those ideas. (AO1/AO2)

Start with the extract but explain details with references to other parts of the play. (AO3)

Stay relevant to the question focus: how Macbeth both resists and uses the supernatural. (AO1)

Here are some ideas that could be included in an answer to this question and which cover the Assessment Objectives (AOs):

AO1 The witches and Macbeth try to use each other. Is he a victim of evil? Do evil forces control and corrupt him? Note how Shakespeare shows us who has the upper hand at times during the play.

AO2 Note the strength of Macbeth's words (which suggest violence and scorn) here and elsewhere. He changes through the play, as do audience reactions to him. Compare the witches' sarcasm and trickery with Macbeth's own scorn ('Filthy hags!').

AO3 Consider significance of differences between contemporary and modern beliefs about evil and the supernatural.

A student has decided to focus on the power struggle between Macbeth and evil spirits. This is the plan they have made to answer the question. Note how the student intends to compare the extract to other parts of the play throughout their answer.

Paragraph	Content		Timing
1	Intro - use the question prep (see above) to establish focus of answer, and my key idea – relationship as power struggle		9.40
2	Explore extract – evidence of the type of relationship		9.43
3	What witches' **language** suggests about their relationship/ attitude	Refer back to the extract and question focus throughout. Question the 'relationship' with the supernatural and what Shakespeare might be **implying**.	9.58
4	Witches' attitude to Macbeth revealed elsewhere		10.06
5	How Macbeth invokes **imagery** of evil and the supernatural elsewhere		10.14
6	Conclusion – brief return to question/would a modern audience be willing to see Macbeth as a victim of evil forces? (villain/victim)		10.22

The essay plan above will meet these Assessment Objectives:

AO1 Read, understand and respond	Explore the relationship between Macbeth and the supernatural, considering how Shakespeare might want the audience to react. Use evidence to support insights.
AO2 Language, form and structure	Close look at how Macbeth's attitudes are reflected in his language. How the relationship changes/becomes fully revealed during the play.
AO3 Contexts	The relevance of contemporary and modern assumptions about the powers of witches. Location of extract in **context** of whole play.

The relationship between Macbeth and supernatural forces is complex[1] and is made more complicated by the different sets of assumptions that contemporary and modern audiences are likely to bring with them to the performance. Most people in the early 17th century believed not only in the existence of witches, but also in their ability to corrupt a good man into doing evil. Modern audiences are likely to be sceptical.[2]

In this extract, Macbeth tries to intimidate the witches one moment (calling them 'filthy hags')[3] and is defeatist the next when he fears that the Banquo family's hold on the crown will 'stretch out to the crack of doom'[3] – his own. This veering between scornful insults and pathetic pessimism is typical of Macbeth[4]. Here, Macbeth wants the witches to give him hard information, yet he responds with the **rhetorical question**, 'Why do you show me this?', as though he wants the witches to tell him only what he wants to hear. It is as though he is trying to force the witches into a relationship of flattering courtiers or servants.[5]

The witches' aim, however, is to torment Macbeth[6] – to 'grieve his heart' – not to be his servants. Shakespeare lets us know this before the witches show Macbeth the future, so we watch Macbeth's reactions with the witches' aims in mind.[6] Therefore, when Macbeth cries, 'Start, eyes!', we know that he would rather tear out his own eyes than understand what the witches are telling him, but we also know that the witches are enjoying his torment:[6] they are in command. When the 'show of kings' is over, Macbeth asks 'What, is this so?' His question shows that he no longer considers himself all-knowing and all-powerful.[7] Now he is almost pleading with the witches. That suggests he is now inferior[7] in his relationship to them. The witches then put on a show for Macbeth to cheer him up. Their cruel sarcasm and insensitivity to Macbeth's dilemma is conveyed by their inappropriate choice of word, 'delights'. Their verbal cruelty emphasises the power they now have over him: Macbeth thought he could use the witches, but in fact they are toying with him for their own amusement.[8]

We should not be surprised at the witches' cunning and cruelty:[9] in an earlier scene their boss, Hecate, told the witches that their aim should be to use spirits to 'draw him [Macbeth] on to his confusion' – his downfall. The witches' cunning allows them to enjoy tempting people – including Macbeth – to destroy themselves. Macbeth fails to fully recognise the witches' strength[9] that comes from their magic and probably from their 'sisterhood'. Both of these sources of strength are suggested to the audience in those scenes where the witches gather round chanting and making spells.[9] At such times, the witches' hypnotic **rhythms** and **rhymes**, repetitions and their shared chants make it very clear that they are

[1] **AO1:** clear opening, using words from the question to ensure relevance.

[2] **AO1/AO3:** 'conceptual' approach – question focus viewed from POV of differences between audiences in different ages.

[3] **AO1:** deft choices of details to support points.

[4] **AO3:** Macbeth's behaviour here set in context of whole play.

[5] **AO1/AO2:** apt quotation explored for its significance ('It is as though...').

[6] **AO1:** subtle development of analysis of how Shakespeare presents the relationship.

[7] **AO2:** insight into how Shakespeare develops our understanding of the relationship and how it changes (**structure**).

[8] **AO1/AO2:** an exploratory response and sensitivity to language and form is leading to deeper insights into the relationship.

[9] **AO1/AO3:** knowledge of whole play leads to greater appreciation of aspects of the extract.

completely united and confident. Their controlled, as if pre-rehearsed, language[10] in these scenes contrasts strongly with Macbeth's own wild imagery and his rants, which are powerful but suggest much less order and control[10] than the witches always display.

> [10] **AO2**: clear understanding of how Shakespeare uses form to shape meaning and **effect**.

Macbeth's problem is that he has a fatal attraction to the forces of evil. For example, when he refers to Banquo's planned murder he seems to go into a trance of evil with his images drawn from darkness and witchcraft: such as, 'the crow makes wing to the rooky wood', and he talks of the work of 'night's black agents'. His lines are rhythmic and in **rhyming couplets**, as though he is a magician creating a wicked spell.[10] The trouble is that although he thinks he is now all-powerful, the witches are deceiving him and leading him into a trap.[11]

> [11] **AO1**: further development of idea that supernatural forces are the stronger partner in the relationship.

So, is Macbeth just a helpless victim? The relationship is unequal: Macbeth is deceived and ignorant; the witches are clear-sighted and all-knowing. If you believe in witches and their spells – as many did in Shakespeare's time – then you are likely to sympathise with Macbeth. Modern audiences are more likely to condemn Macbeth as a greedy, brutal 'monster' or 'butcher'.[12]

> [12] **AO3**: useful understanding of the impact of context on a modern audience's reactions.

Commentary

This is a critical, exploratory response that develops a relevant and well-structured line of inquiry. The answer is based on profound insights, especially in relation to the concept of 'context'. A range of deftly chosen details clarifies insights into the relationship between language, form and meaning. **Subject terminology** is used accurately and usefully to support concise analysis.

DO IT!

Now use what you've learned to answer the following AQA exam-style question.

Read the extract from Act 4 Scene 1 of *Macbeth* on page 6.

Starting with this moment in the play, explore how Shakespeare presents feelings of guilt in *Macbeth*.

Write about:

- how Shakespeare presents feelings of guilt in this extract
- how Shakespeare presents feelings of guilt in the play as a whole.

[30 marks]
AO4 [4 marks]

Read the following extract from Act 3 Scene 4 of *Macbeth* and then answer the question that follows.

At this point in the play, Lady Macbeth reassures their guests about Macbeth's behaviour.

LADY MACBETH
Sit, worthy friends; my lord is often thus,
And hath been from his youth. Pray you, keep seat.
The fit is momentary; upon a thought
He will again be well. If much you note him,
5   You shall offend him and extend his passion.
Feed, and regard him not. – Are you a man?

MACBETH
Ay, and a bold one, that dare look on that
Which might appal the devil.

LADY MACBETH
O proper stuff!
10   This is the very painting of your fear;
This is the air-drawn dagger which you said
Led you to Duncan. O, these flaws and starts,
Impostors to true fear, would well become
A woman's story at a winter's fire,
15   Authorized by her grandam. Shame itself!
Why do you make such faces? When all's done,
You look but on a stool.

MACBETH
Prithee, see there! Behold! Look! Lo! How say you?
Why, what care I? If thou canst nod, speak too.
20   If charnel houses and our graves must send
Those that we bury back, our monuments
Shall be the maws of kites.

Exit GHOST.

LADY MACBETH
What, quite unmann'd in folly?

MACBETH
If I stand here, I saw him.

LADY MACBETH
25   Fie, for shame!

Starting with this moment in the play, explore how far Shakespeare presents Lady Macbeth as a loyal and supportive partner to Macbeth.

Write about:

- how Shakespeare presents Lady Macbeth at this moment in the play

- how far Shakespeare presents Lady Macbeth as a loyal and supportive partner in the play as a whole.

[30 marks]
AO4 [4 marks]

Zoom in on the question

Starting with this moment in the play, explore how far Shakespeare presents Lady Macbeth as a loyal and supportive partner to Macbeth.

Write about:

- how Shakespeare presents Macbeth at this moment in the play
- how Shakespeare presents Lady Macbeth as a loyal and supportive partner in the play as a whole.

Focus on the extract before expanding your response to the rest of the play.

The play is a construct written by Shakespeare; it is not showing 'real life'.

The focus for the essay. You are analysing how far you believe Lady Macbeth is 'loyal and supportive'. (AO1)

This refers to the language choices and methods Shakespeare uses. (AO2)

Expand your answer to include the whole of the play.

Focus on the significance of the extract – in this case it is a turning point for Macbeth. (AO1)

Here are some ideas that could be included in an answer to this question and which cover the Assessment Objectives (AOs):

AO1 Evidence of Lady Macbeth seeking to manage both the guests' reactions to Macbeth's behaviour and Macbeth's reactions to the apparition (either real or in his head). Is she still loyal to him? Is she supportive of him or is she irritated and annoyed? Are her reactions as a result of her own quest for power?

AO2 Examine the difference between Lady Macbeth's public soothing and her hard, scornful language in the extract and in other parts of the play. How does Macbeth's language towards his wife change during the course of the play?

AO3 Consider women as 'power behind the throne' rather than powerful in their own right. Would a modern audience accept this view? What would a contemporary audience think about Lady Macbeth's behaviour towards Macbeth? Would they find her sharp responses unusual?

A student has decided to focus on the difference between Lady Macbeth's loyalty and support given to Macbeth at the start of the play and how far she can be seen as supportive in this extract.

Paragraph	Content	Timing
1	Intro – use the question preparation to establish focus and my key idea – Lady M behaviours and how they link to theme of appearance and reality	9.40
2	Evidence of Lady M being helpful in the extract – supporting M from embarrassment and discovery. Also of her harsh attitude towards him.	9.43
3	Lady M's attitudes seen through Shakespeare's language. Audience reaction to this.	9.58
4	Compare attitudes with Act I Scene 5 when Lady M hears about the witches' predictions.	10.06
5	Loyalty – evidence and what inspires it? Love? Lady M's ambitions for Macbeth and her place in society as 'woman behind the throne'.	10.14
6	Evidence of Lady M and M's partnership and how it dissolves by the end of the play.	10.22

The essay plan above will meet these Assessment Objectives:

AO1 Read, understand and respond	Lady Macbeth appears loyal when she speaks to guests, but her language has a different **tone** when speaking privately to Macbeth. Using supportive evidence, consider how Shakespeare might want the audience to react.
AO2 Language, form and structure	Examples of language to support an **interpretation** of Lady Macbeth's early partnership and growing distance from Macbeth. Her use of **rhetoric** to manipulate and control Macbeth. How their relationship changes.
AO3 Contexts	The relevance of contemporary and modern views of the status and place of women in power.

The relationship between Macbeth and Lady Macbeth [1] sits at the heart of Shakespeare's play and develops as the couple's fortune changes. Throughout the play we see the couple falsifying evidence to present their version of reality to the other **characters**. In this extract, we see Lady Macbeth presenting [2] a version of reality to support and protect Macbeth.

The extract is taken from the scene where Macbeth, now king, sees (or believes he sees) Banquo's ghost. Shakespeare presents Lady Macbeth supportively, [3] managing Macbeth's reputation as she simultaneously manages his behaviour. The audience sees her as reassuring Macbeth that this is 'the very painting' of his 'fear'. Here we see her loyalty as she tries to soothe and calm Macbeth, as well as ensuring the other characters accept her version of reality. Within the extract, [4] she publicly shows her support for Macbeth in front of their guests, yet the private rebukes, 'Shame itself', shows the relationship's development from support to manipulation to 'shame'. Significantly, Lady Macbeth's use of 'shame' foreshadows the dishonour Macbeth brings to his name, contrasting with 'worthy' Macbeth in Act 1.

At the start of the extract, Lady Macbeth appears loyal when she tries to save Macbeth's reputation by telling the 'worthy friends' that he is 'often thus' and has been from 'his youth'. This language of flattery, [5] 'worthy', and the assurance that this is normal for Macbeth clearly signals her supportive reassurance. However, this quickly changes as she addresses Macbeth privately within the same line with the question, 'Are you a man?' The audience will recognise Lady Macbeth's use of this line of questioning from the first act of the play. There we see her question his manliness when he waivers in his intent to kill Duncan, saying that he would be 'a man' when 'durst you do it'. Once again, in the extract, [6] we see her link his actions to his public persona as a warrior and king. However, this change between the public supportive language and private harsh words could lead the audience to question her loyalty. Shakespeare presents Lady Macbeth's disdain as she scoffs, 'O proper stuff!', the exclamation showing her scorn and her desire for him to temper his reactions.

In Act 1, where Lady Macbeth responds to Macbeth's letter, we see her loyalty and ambition for Macbeth as she calls on 'you spirits' to 'unsex me here' and fill her with 'direst cruelty'. Both a modern and a contemporary audience would recognise how this reveals Lady Macbeth's support for Macbeth's ambition, as her direct language and imagery [7] – 'take my milk for gall' – is also shown through her use of **monosyllables** ('gall', 'hell', 'peep'), which reinforce her decisiveness. Her loyalty to his ambition is seen in Lady Macbeth's desire to suppress these feminine traits, as these traits

1 AO1: 'conceptual' approach – interpretation of the centrality of the relationship between the Macbeths and how this develops.

2 AO1: using words from the question.

3 AO2: deft summary of evidence to support key idea.

4 AO1/AO2: evidence deftly chosen and subtleties of meaning explained.

5 AO2: precise and helpful use of subject terminology, with perceptive comments on the effects of specific techniques.

6 AO1: perceptive analysis of concept of public/private and its significance to the action.

7 AO2: precise and helpful use of subject terminology, with perceptive comments on the effects of specific techniques.

were linked with weakness. Perhaps this is why she shows her scorn for any similar signs of weakness from Macbeth.

A modern audience[8] might question what inspires Lady Macbeth's love for Macbeth: is it true love or is the relationship based on her own ambition? Certainly, a contemporary audience would recognise the idea of the woman as the power behind the throne and would be familiar with this view of the role of women as supporting a man in power without wielding power directly. A modern audience, perhaps seeing this differently, would also consider the complexity of a woman struggling to reconcile her ambition for her husband with the reality of the man he has transformed into as his power and influence has grown.

By the time the extract takes place in the play, Lady Macbeth's position as a 'partner in greatness' has changed. It is through Banquo's murder that we see Macbeth acting alone – without the support of his wife. Earlier, Shakespeare presents Lady Macbeth jointly planning Duncan's murder with Macbeth, showing her central role in the murder and her commitment to Macbeth's advancement. By the murder of Banquo, however,[9] Lady Macbeth is sidelined, with no knowledge of the events. In fact, by the end of the play, her death is met with Macbeth's dismissive, 'She should have died hereafter'. The audience sees how the loyalty and support[10] of his 'dearest partner in greatness' is swept aside by the corrupting nature of power.

[8] **AO3**: perceptive comments on the play's impact on modern audiences.

[9] **AO3**: consideration of themes in the extract, enriched by comparing their treatment in other parts of the play.

[10] **AO1**: here the insight into the relationship between loyalty and power is reinforced.

Commentary

This is a thoughtful response that develops a relevant and systematic answer to the question. Some perceptive and revealing links are made between the play and relevant contexts, with exploration of the reactions of a modern and contemporary audience to Lady Macbeth's language.

DO IT!

Now use what you've learned to answer the following AQA exam-style question.

Read the extract from Act 3 Scene 4 of *Macbeth* on page 10.

Starting with this moment in the play, explore how Shakespeare presents ideas about the relationship between Macbeth and Banquo in *Macbeth*.

Write about:

- how Shakespeare presents ideas about the relationship between Macbeth and Banquo at this moment in the play
- how Shakespeare presents ideas about the relationship between Macbeth and Banquo in the play as a whole.

[30 marks]
AO4 [4 marks]

Read the following extract from Act 1 Scene 2 of *Macbeth* and then answer the question that follows.

At this point in the play, a wounded captain brings King Duncan a report from the battlefield.

MALCOLM
                    Hail, brave friend!
Say to the King the knowledge of the broil
As thou didst leave it.

SERGEANT
Doubtful it stood,
5   As two spent swimmers that do cling together
And choke their art. The merciless Macdonwald –
Worthy to be a rebel, for to that
The multiplying villainies of nature
Do swarm upon him – from the Western Isles
10 Of kerns and gallowglasses is supplied;
And Fortune, on his damned quarrel smiling,
Show'd like a rebel's whore. But all's too weak;
For brave Macbeth – well he deserves that name –
Disdaining Fortune, with his brandish'd steel,
15 Which smoked with bloody execution,
Like Valour's minion carved out his passage
Till he faced the slave,
Which ne'er shook hands, nor bade farewell to him,
Till he unseam'd him from the nave to the chaps,
20 And fix'd his head upon our battlements.

DUNCAN
O valiant cousin! Worthy gentleman!

Starting with this extract, explore how Shakespeare presents Macbeth as a brave man in *Macbeth*.

Write about:

- how Shakespeare presents Macbeth in this extract

- how Shakespeare presents Macbeth as a brave man in the play as a whole.

[30 marks]
AO4 [4 marks]

Zoom in on the question

Starting with this extract, explore how Shakespeare presents Macbeth as a brave man in *Macbeth*.

Write about:

- how Shakespeare presents Macbeth in this extract
- how Shakespeare presents Macbeth as a brave man in the play as a whole.

Establish evidence of bravery in this extract and compare Macbeth here with elsewhere in the play. (AO2)

How Shakespeare uses language and dramatic structure to shape the audience's response to Macbeth. (AO1)

AO3: (a) placing the extract in the context of the whole play; (b) Macbeth as a public hero.

Theme/character focus for the question. (AO1)

Here are some ideas that could be included in an answer to this question and which cover the Assessment Objectives (AOs):

AO1 Macbeth risks his life for his king and country. He is brave throughout the play, especially at the end, but he is also afraid, violent, treacherous, and even cowardly. Macduff calls him a coward near the end. Consider this view as opposite to brave. Compare with Lady Macbeth's warning of the danger of Macbeth being too cowardly to take what he deserves.

AO2 Brave both at the beginning and end, despite other characteristics. Shakespeare uses this circular structure to emphasise Macbeth's bravery. Much of the language suggests determination and single-mindedness (bravery). See extract and Macbeth's language of defiance in face of overwhelming odds ('Blow wind, come wrack'; 'I will not yield').

AO3 Bravery and manliness/heroism reinforce each other. How do we tend to estimate 'bravery'? Can you be brave and bad?

A student has decided to focus on Macbeth's bravery and heroism. This is the plan they have made to answer the question. Note how the student intends to compare the extract to other parts of the play throughout their answer.

Paragraph	Content		Timing
1	Intro – use the question prep to establish focus of answer, and my key angle: Macbeth's heroism.		9.40
2	Explore extract – evidence of heroic bravery/approval.		9.47
3	Other early evidence of Macbeth's bravery and heroism. Focus on AO2 language.	Refer back to extract and question focus throughout. Question what Shakespeare might be implying about Macbeth's character.	10.02
4	How Macbeth is presented in Act 5 (including how manliness interacts with bravery and heroism).		10.13
5	Conclusion – is Macbeth a brave hero or a cowardly villain?		10.22

The essay plan above will meet these Assessment Objectives:

AO1 Read, understand and respond	Aspects of Macbeth's character and how bravery compares with other aspects. How Shakespeare shapes our reaction to Macbeth.
AO2 Language, form and structure	Explore how Macbeth is presented (a) at different points in the play, for example his discussions with LM, his behaviour linked to Banquo's murder, his defence of his castle in Act 5; (b) in the language used about him in Act 1 (including extract).
AO3 Contexts	How bravery/heroism/patriotism mask other aspects of Macbeth and promote approval of him (including by audience).

Clearly, in many ways Macbeth is very brave:[1] he is willing to give up his own life for his king and country and in battle he fights with no regard for his own personal safety. Of course, from other points of view, he is treacherous, scared, violent, and even cowardly. However, whatever he does during the play, his bravery is still on show at the end, so that even at his most murderous and bloodthirsty, Shakespeare allows us to admire him. But perhaps any admiration we do still have for him at the end is based not just on his bravery and determination, but also on the heroism and patriotism that his bravery supports.[2] He may be a 'dead butcher' at the end, but he started out as a brave and selfless patriot.

On the surface the captain's report is full of admiration and presents Macbeth as very brave indeed: he is 'brave Macbeth' who definitely 'deserves that name'. He 'disdains fortune.'[3] 'Disdain' has a theatrical effect: it conveys Macbeth as so contemptuous of his enemy's fighting abilities that he can 'turn his nose up' at it. Macbeth fights on against all odds with no regard for the danger to him personally. His bravery is emphasised by his decisiveness and by the force he uses, suggesting he puts himself right into the thick of the battle, fighting his way through the rebel army until he reached Macdonald and hacked him to pieces.[4] The captain admires Macbeth for being 'Valour's minion' – meaning that he was bravery **personified**: he was nothing but bravery through and through.[5] We might begin to worry that a taste for brutality explains Macbeth more than bravery does, except that the captain describes Macbeth's bloody sword as an instrument of 'execution': this casts Macbeth as a bringer of justice, not a murderous thug.[6] Duncan is impressed and hails Macbeth 'O valiant cousin!', but then perhaps complimenting someone for being brave was just a convention because Duncan routinely greeted the captain as 'brave friend' as soon as he arrived.[6] Whatever the case, the overall impression of Macbeth given by the sergeant's report is someone who is brave in the service of his king, his country and justice. He is a hero.[7]

Ross's report from the battlefield confirms Macbeth's bravery and how it led to 'victory'. The important point is that we learn all this before Macbeth has even appeared on stage. When he does turn up we automatically react to him from our image of him as a ferocious, brave and loyal warrior – a war hero. Later in Act 1, when his wife taunts Macbeth for being a 'coward' who is 'all talk and no do', too afraid to do what he has to do (murder Duncan) to get what he wants (the throne), we know this is not really true: in battle he was willing to sacrifice his own life for what he believed in – king and country.[8]

[1] **AO1:** clear opening, using words from the question to ensure relevance.

[2] **AO1/AO3:** 'conceptual' approach – question focus viewed from POV of importance of links between bravery and heroism.

[3] **AO1:** deft choices of details to support points.

[4] **AO1/AO2:** very relevant analysis of the text, summarising telling details in support.

[5] **AO1:** quotation explained well.

[6] **AO1/AO2:** appreciation of significance of small details of language choice.

[7] **AO1:** deft summing up of relevant aspect of Macbeth's heroism.

[8] **AO1/AO3:** knowledge of whole play and consideration of audience response leads to deeper appreciation of significance of the extract.

Even in Act 5, after Macbeth finally realises the **dramatic irony** of the witches' predictions, he fights on hopelessly rather than surrender. 'I will not yield' he tells Macduff. The **phrase** 'will not' literally confirms the strength of his will, his refusal to ever give up. However, when he is finally killed, Malcolm calls him 'this dead butcher' (a **metaphor** that completes the captain's battle image: that Macbeth 'carv'd out his passage') and this condemnation makes us wonder if all along Macbeth has been not brave, but just a savage thug.[9]

Physically Macbeth is certainly brave, but by the end of the play he is no longer a national hero: the new and rightful king hails Macbeth's death as the saving of Scotland from 'tyranny'. Macbeth's bravery has been put to a very wrong use, and 'wrong' bravery is no bravery at all.[10]

[9] **AO2 (structure):** clear understanding of how development of action and imagery through the play help Shakespeare to shape meaning and effect.

[10] **AO1/AO3:** clear insight into difference between physical and moral bravery provides conclusion to questions raised in the introduction.

Commentary

This is a critical and thoughtful response that develops a relevant and systematic answer to the question. This is a conceptualised answer based on subtle insights into aspects of bravery and how Shakespeare presents Macbeth. Some profound insights are provided based on a fine appreciation of language details and how Shakespeare structures our responses to Macbeth through the play. The answer is strengthened by being rooted in a subtle understanding of popular ideas about bravery and heroism.

DO IT!

Now use what you've learned to answer the following AQA exam-style question.

Read the extract from Act 1 Scene 2 of *Macbeth* on page 14.

Starting with this conversation, explore how Shakespeare presents aggression in *Macbeth*.

Write about:

- how Shakespeare presents aggression in this conversation
- how Shakespeare presents aggression in the play as a whole.

[30 marks]
AO4 [4 marks]

Read the following extract from Act 1 Scene 1 of *Macbeth* and then answer the question that follows.

This is the opening scene of the play. Macbeth and the witches have not met yet.

> *A deserted place. Thunder and lightning.*
> *Enter three* WITCHES.
>
> **FIRST WITCH**
> When shall we three meet again?
> In thunder, lightning, or in rain?
>
> **SECOND WITCH**
> When the hurlyburly's done,
> When the battle's lost and won.
>
> **THIRD WITCH**
> 5   That will be ere the set of sun.
>
> **FIRST WITCH**
> Where the place?
>
> **SECOND WITCH**
> Upon the heath.
>
> **THIRD WITCH**
> There to meet with Macbeth.
>
> **FIRST WITCH**
> I come, Graymalkin.
>
> **SECOND WITCH**
> 10   Paddock calls.
>
> **THIRD WITCH**
> Anon!
>
> **ALL**
> Fair is foul, and foul is fair.
> Hover through the fog and filthy air.
>
> *Exeunt.*

Starting with this extract, explore how Shakespeare presents evil and the supernatural in *Macbeth*.

Write about:

- how Shakespeare presents evil and the supernatural in this extract
- how Shakespeare presents evil and the supernatural in the play as a whole.

[30 marks]
AO4 [4 marks]

Zoom in on the question

Starting with this extract, explore how Shakespeare presents evil and the supernatural in *Macbeth*.

Write about:

- how Shakespeare presents evil and the supernatural in this extract

- how Shakespeare presents evil and the supernatural in the play as a whole.

Focus on the extract, to 'anchor' the question and explore some details about evil and the supernatural.

Concentrate on Shakespeare's ideas about evil and the supernatural and how he chooses to present these ideas. (AO1)

Start with the extract but clarify/explain details with references to the whole play.

This is the question focus. Stay relevant to it. Refer to 'evil' and 'supernatural' elements in the play to help you stay on track. (AO1/2)

Here are some ideas that could be included in an answer to this question and which cover the Assessment Objectives (AOs):

AO1 The play is full of supernatural elements, but to what extent is Shakespeare suggesting they are to blame for Macbeth's actions or what happens to him? Are these elements real or the product of tormented and guilty minds? Consider the tension between supernatural/evil elements and evil deeds – to what extent are the witches to blame for the evil in the play?

AO2 How is the supernatural mood created in the extract through the rhythm and **rhyme** used by the witches and Shakespeare's language choices, especially the last two lines? Compare the witches' language and tone with that of Macbeth and Lady Macbeth as they evoke the powers of witchcraft. Consider how the opening of the play sets a tone of cruelty and evil.

AO3 Consider the significance of King James I's public attitudes towards witchcraft and how Shakespeare might be drawing on these. How would audiences react to this?

A student has decided to focus on Shakespeare's use of supernatural elements. This is the plan they have made to answer the question. Note how the student intends to compare the extract to other parts of the play throughout their answer.

Paragraph	Content		Timing
1	Intro – use the question prep to establish focus of answer, and my key idea – is this evil as a force or evil actions by characters?		9.40
2	Explore extract – focus on how the setting sets the tone, and the impact of this opening on audiences.		9.43
3	How Shakespeare's language choices establish supernatural mood in opening scene; open out to further examples in play.	Refer back to extract and question focus throughout.	9.58
4	The fascination of the supernatural and witches for audiences. King James I's fear of witches.		10.06
5	To what extent are witches to blame for evil that pervades play?		10.14
6	Conclusion: how far is supernatural world to blame for the fate of the Macbeths?		10.22

The essay plan above will meet these Assessment Objectives:

AO1 Read, understand and respond	Explore how Shakespeare uses the supernatural and evil to set the tone of the play and guide the audience's response to M and LM's actions. Consider whether evil is presented as a force or evil actions by characters.
AO2 Language, form and structure	Explore language choices in the extract, for example the language of spells and prediction, and how these might set the tone of the play. Compare with examples from Lady Macbeth and Macbeth elsewhere in the play.
AO3 Contexts	Compare contemporary and modern audiences' reactions to evil and supernatural events.

In *Macbeth*, Shakespeare presents a world where the supernatural world and the natural world[1] overlap, where witches and their potions predict events and apparitions haunt the king with the horror of 'screams of death'.

The extract opens the play. Given that the play charts the rise and fall of the eponymous hero, the audience could rightly expect to meet Macbeth in the opening scene. Instead,[2] the audience is taken to a 'deserted place' where we meet 'three witches'. Immediately Shakespeare plunges us into this strange world with its cruel and evil acts, where Macbeth and his battle are discussed. This opening, with its 'Thunder and lightning', immediately alerts the audience to the prominence of evil and the supernatural while also linking Macbeth's name to this world. In this opening scene, the witches take centre stage. Their opening line of questioning, 'When shall we three meet again?', connects the audience to their world, the adverb 'again' implying that these meetings have already happened and will continue to happen repeatedly. This prophetic[3] language, coupled with its **trochaic meter** creates ominous drum-like rhythms, drawing the audience into the witches' spell as they talk of 'when the battle's lost and won'.

This supernatural atmosphere[4] develops further through the witches' references to their familiars, 'Graymalkin' and 'Paddock', a recognisable concept for all audiences. Their celebration of 'foul' and evil actions is emphasised by the rhythm[5] of the line 'Fair is foul, and foul is fair' as it chants its rejection of 'fair' and good elements. The use of rhyme in 'fair/air' makes it an incantation, a spell, and Shakespeare's juxtaposition of 'foul' and 'fair' signals how these characters will hide their true intentions throughout the play. The audience is further alerted to these intentions in Act 1 Scene 3 when Macbeth uses these very words when we meet him for the first time, 'So foul and fair a day I have not seen'. Before Macbeth[6] enters, the witches declare that the 'charm's wound up', suggesting that through their spells they have lured Macbeth, taking control of him. Conversely here, Shakespeare's use of 'meet with Macbeth' suggests that Macbeth is in some part complicit in this action. At the end of the extract, the **alliterative** 'fog and filthy' links the witches with air through the insubstantial 'f' sounds, foreshadowing the predictions that will steer the action of the play and establishing the tone of cruel evil from its outset.

Through the prominence of the witches in the first scene[7] and their significance in driving the **plot** forward, it appears that Shakespeare is drawing on King James I's attitudes towards witchcraft. It can be no coincidence that both Macbeth and Lady Macbeth use the language of

[1] **AO1**: clear opening, using words from the question to ensure relevance.

[2] **AO2**: insight into Shakespeare's craft as a dramatist.

[3] **AO1/AO2**: relevant analysis of the text, summarising telling details to support analysis including reference to trochaic meter (a stressed syllable followed by an unstressed syllable).

[4] **AO1/AO3**: consideration of audience response leads to deeper appreciation of the extract's significance.

[5] **AO2**: relevant use of subject terminology.

[6] **AO1/AO3**: knowledge of whole play leads to deeper appreciation of the extract's significance.

[7] **AO1/AO3**: perceptive summing up of significance of the theme, especially to contemporary audiences.

witchcraft and 'horror' as they plan the murder of Duncan. Shakespeare presents Macbeth calling on the skies to hide his 'black' desires and Lady Macbeth calls on the spirits to 'unsex' her by ridding her of any feminine, merciful traits. With King James'[8] fear of regicide, Shakespeare is perhaps showing the King and the audience that this crime is linked with evil and supernatural forces causing mental torment to anyone who distorts the natural order of God's will.

[8] AO3: excellent reference to contemporary beliefs to deepen understanding of the role of the supernatural in the play.

Shakespeare presents a world where the natural order has been disrupted by Duncan's death, triggering a chain of 'unnatural' supernatural events. Ross tells of 'darkness' that 'strangles' and entombs daylight.[9] These violent images evoke the horror of these disturbances in nature. This violence is seen again as Duncan's 'beauteous' horses 'Turn'd wild' as if to make 'War with mankind'. Shakespeare presents Macbeth's 'fatal vision' of a 'dagger' as he makes his way to Duncan's chamber and his horror when he believes he sees Banquo's ghost with its 'gory locks', a projection of the guilt that is tormenting him. Shakespeare presents evil and witchcraft triggering this alarming breakdown in the natural world. However, it is Macbeth's ambition and quest for power that allows him to be manipulated by the forces of evil.

[9] AO1/AO3: 'conceptual' approach – question focus viewed from POV of importance of links between supernatural temptation and evil deeds.

Shakespeare presents a world shaken by supernatural events and evil deeds. However, the underlying evil comes from Macbeth's desire for absolute power and the ambition that leads him to commit evil to seize this power. In this, Macbeth reveals himself open to the influence of supernatural beings.

Commentary

This is an exploratory response that develops a relevant and well-developed line of enquiry. The answer pursues key ideas about Macbeth's links to the supernatural, providing a conceptualised approach that is supported by precise choices of textual details and relevant use of subject terminology. Ideas and examples considered in relation to both a contemporary and a modern audience enrich the analysis.

DO IT!

Now use what you've learned to answer the following AQA exam-style question.

Read the extract from Act 1 Scene 1 of *Macbeth* on page 18.

Starting with this extract, write about how Shakespeare explores ideas about appearance and reality in *Macbeth*.

Write about:

- what the witches hint about appearance and reality in this extract
- how Shakespeare explores ideas about appearance and reality in the play as a whole.

[30 marks]
AO4 [4 marks]

Read the following extract from Act 3 Scene 6 of *Macbeth* and then answer the question that follows.

At this point in the play, Lennox and a Lord are discussing the murders of Duncan and Banquo.

Enter LENNOX *and another* LORD.

LENNOX
My former speeches have but hit your thoughts,
Which can interpret further; only I say
Things have been strangely borne. The gracious Duncan
Was pitied of Macbeth; marry, he was dead.
5   And the right valiant Banquo walk'd too late,
Whom, you may say, if't please you, Fleance kill'd,
For Fleance fled. Men must not walk too late.
Who cannot want the thought, how monstrous
It was for Malcolm and for Donalbain
10   To kill their gracious father? Damned fact!
How it did grieve Macbeth! Did he not straight,
In pious rage, the two delinquents tear
That were the slaves of drink and thralls of sleep?
Was not that nobly done? Ay, and wisely too,
15   For 'twould have anger'd any heart alive
To hear the men deny't. So that, I say,
He has borne all things well; and I do think
That, had he Duncan's sons under his key –
As, an't please heaven, he shall not – they should find
20   What 'twere to kill a father; so should Fleance.
But, peace! For from broad words, and 'cause he fail'd
His presence at the tyrant's feast, I hear,
Macduff lives in disgrace.

Starting with this speech, explore how Shakespeare presents one or more of the minor Lords as commentators on the action.

Choose from Lennox, Ross, Angus and/or the unnamed 'Lord' in this scene.

Write about:

- how Shakespeare presents Lennox as a commentator in this speech

- how Shakespeare presents minor Lords as commentators in the play as a whole.

[30 marks]
AO4 [4 marks]

Zoom in on the question

Starting with this speech, explore how Shakespeare presents one or more of the minor Lords as commentators on the action.

Choose from Lennox, Ross, Angus and/or the unnamed 'Lord' in this scene.

Write about:

- how Shakespeare presents Lennox as a commentator in this speech
- how Shakespeare presents minor Lords as commentators in the play as a whole.

Identify the functions of this speech before comparing it with other reports. Establish relevant aspects of the Lords' functions. (AO1)

Focus on how Shakespeare uses the Lords within the play's structure. (AO2)

The question's focus (AO1) is the Lords' role within Shakespeare's dramatic techniques. (AO2)

Identify use of Lennox in the extract. (AO2)

Compare with similar or contrasting uses of Lords at other points in the play. (AO3)

Here are some ideas that could be included in an answer to this question and which cover the Assessment Objectives (AOs):

AO1 Shakespeare's varied uses of the Lords as summarisers, commentators, etc and their similarity to Ancient **Greek choruses** at points in the play; for example, when they summarise action we have not seen on stage and guide us in how we might feel about events.

AO2 Analyse effects of Shakespeare's dramatic techniques: off-stage action; (Greek) chorus; how irony is conveyed in the extract.

AO3 How techniques in the extract are used elsewhere in the play. How the play draws on techniques typical to choruses in Ancient Greek drama (which Shakespeare would have been familiar with).

A student has decided to focus on the Lords' different types of commentating. This is the plan they have made to answer the question. Note how the student intends to compare the extract to other parts of the play throughout their answer.

Paragraph	Content		Timing
1	Intro – answer the question in full but without examples.		9.40
2	Explore extract – evidence of different types of commentating/Lennox's ironic tone.		9.46
3	Lords' roles in summarising action in extract and elsewhere.	Keep referring back to extract and question focus. Provide examples of language subtlety/implied meanings.	9.51
4	Lords' roles in creating mood and atmosphere around action in extract and elsewhere.		10.01
5	Lords' roles in guiding audience responses to action in extract and elsewhere. Compare with Greek chorus tradition.		10.10
6	Conclusion – brief return to question. What is the most important role of Ross and Lennox?		10.19

The essay plan above will meet these Assessment Objectives:

AO1 Read, understand and respond	Explore how Shakespeare uses the Lords for different levels of commentary, their most important one being to guide the audience's response. Use details of language and structure to support ideas.
AO2 Language, form and structure	Explore shades of meaning in language choices in the extract, and how these might imply Lennox's irony.
AO3 Contexts	Compare Lennox's role here with those of Ross and Angus elsewhere. Refer to possible influence of tradition of Greek chorus.

The Lords, particularly Ross and Lennox, are characters in themselves, but Shakespeare also uses them as <u>convenient commentators on the action</u>.❶ Roughly, their commentary operates at three levels: they summarise action that has taken place off stage; they provide atmosphere and 'colour' to these off-stage events so as to increase their significance and dramatic impact for the audience; and – most importantly – <u>they guide the audience in how they should think and feel about the action</u>.❷ Therefore, their commentating role amounts to something quite complex and it enhances the play's dramatic impact rather than just being an optional 'add-on'. Their contribution to the plot is perhaps not absolutely essential, but a <u>director can use these characters</u>❸ to emphasise the play's mystery and drama.

These three levels of commentary can all be found in Lennox's speech. He <u>summarises the basic facts</u>❹ surrounding the murders of Duncan and Banquo and what the evidence seems to reveal about the murderers and the circumstances of the crimes: for example, we are reminded that Malcolm and Donalbain, and Fleance, are all suspected of killing their own fathers. At the second level, <u>Lennox confirms</u>❹ the disgust that everyone feels about these crimes and the criminals. For example, Duncan's murder is '<u>monstrous' and his sons are 'delinquents'</u>.❺ Meanwhile, Lennox's obvious <u>sarcasm shows</u>❹ the audience that Macbeth is not as free from suspicion as he and his wife were hoping to be.

The play very intensely focuses on the Macbeths, their thoughts, feelings and plans. As a result it is difficult for the audience to understand what sort of ruler Macbeth is, how he is viewed by his people and by England, and how much time is passing. Shakespeare uses the Lords to summarise <u>these broader aspects of the action so that he can maintain claustrophobic attention on the Macbeths</u>❻ and their crimes and obsessions. In the extract, for example, we learn the <u>important information that neither Fleance nor Macduff have been captured and that this is a threat to Macbeth.</u>❼ <u>Other Lords give us important information at other times in the play:</u>❽ for example, near the end, Angus reports that there are 'revolts' (rebellions) against Macbeth in Scotland (which will make his defeat easier), and of course Shakespeare avoids the need for a battle scene on-stage at the start of the play by having Ross (and the captain) summarise the battle for us.

Of course, the Lords' summaries are not merely factual: Shakespeare <u>colours them with dramatic and poetic detail to satisfy the audience.</u>❾ For example, Lennox's account of the storm that raged while Macbeth killed

---

❶ **AO1:** clear opening, using words from the question to ensure relevance.

❷ **AO1/AO3:** 'conceptual' approach – Lords as commentators who guide the audience's reactions.

❸ **AO3:** insight into performance as context for the play.

❹ **AO1:** concise explanation of how the 'three levels of comment' are used in this extract.

❺ **AO1:** deft choices of details to support points.

❻ **AO2:** insight into Shakespeare's craft as a dramatist.

❼ **AO1:** precise choice of indirect references to illustrate points.

❽ **AO3:** comparison of use of techniques in the extract and in the play as a whole.

❾ **AO2:** insight into how Shakespeare develops the commentary technique during the play (structure).

Duncan is loaded with dramatic **hyperbole**.[10] Similarly, Ross's battlefield report is loaded with rhetorical repetition[10] (for example, 'point against point') and makes Duncan wait until (after a dramatic pause) Ross reveals they won. The lame anticlimax of his final statement contrasts with, and draws attention to, the **melodramatic** nature of his and the captain's reports.

The most interesting use of the Lords as commentators is when they act like a Greek chorus (a technique that Shakespeare also used in *Romeo and Juliet*) to guide the audience's response.[11] We see this most clearly in the extract where Lennox comments ironically on events: 'Men must not walk too late', he concludes about Banquo's murder, as though that is the most important point.[12] He excuses Macbeth's killing of Duncan's guards as 'pious' and 'noble', but when Lennox goes on to call it 'wise too', we understand that he is hinting that he suspects Macbeth did it to destroy the evidence against him.

Lennox and the other Lords' most important role for Shakespeare might be to summarise important off-stage action, but it is fascinating how often their summaries are likely to unsettle those characters listening – especially Macbeth. Possibly Shakespeare intends these commentators to provoke the audience and deepen their responses to the action. Perhaps all these commentators are there to 'hit [the audience's] thoughts/ Which can interpret further'; they are there to place doubts and to raise questions in audiences' minds.[13]

[10] **AO2**: deft and relevant use of subject terminology.

[11] **AO3**: reference to context of relevant drama conventions and other work by Shakespeare enriches the analysis of the Lords as commentators.

[12] **AO2**: insight into how meaning is implied by tone and choice of language.

[13] **AO3**: sharp understanding of the relationship between **playwright** and audience.

Commentary

This is an exploratory and profound response with a relevant and well-developed line of enquiry. The answer pursues a conceptualised approach that is supported by precise choices of textual details and relevant use of subject terminology. The analysis is enriched by ideas and examples being considered in relation to a number of revealing contexts, including the full text, dramatic conventions and performance.

DO IT!

Now use what you've learned to answer the following AQA exam-style question.

Read the extract from Act 3 Scene 6 of *Macbeth* on page 22.

Starting with this speech, write about how Shakespeare explores suspicion in *Macbeth*.

Write about:

- what Lennox hints about suspicion in this speech
- how Shakespeare explores suspicion in the play as a whole.

[30 marks]
AO4 [4 marks]

Read the following extract from Act 2 Scene 3 of *Macbeth* and then answer the question that follows.

At this point in the play, Macduff and Lennox have just arrived at the Macbeths' castle. Macduff has gone to Duncan's chamber.

> **LENNOX**
> The night has been unruly. Where we lay,
> Our chimneys were blown down, and, as they say,
> Lamentings heard i' the air, strange screams of death,
> And prophesying with accents terrible
> 5   Of dire combustion and confused events
> New hatch'd to the woeful time. The obscure bird
> Clamour'd the livelong night. Some say the earth
> Was feverous and did shake.
>
> **MACBETH**
> 'Twas a rough night.
>
> **LENNOX**
> 10 My young remembrance cannot parallel
> A fellow to it.
>
> *Re-enter MACDUFF.*
>
> **MACDUFF**
> O horror, horror, horror! Tongue nor heart
> Cannot conceive nor name thee.
>
> **MACBETH and LENNOX**
> What's the matter?
>
> **MACDUFF**
> 15 Confusion now hath made his masterpiece.
> Most sacrilegious murder hath broke ope
> The Lord's anointed temple and stole thence
> The life o' the building.
>
> **MACBETH**
> What is't you say? the life?
>
> **LENNOX**
> 20 Mean you his Majesty?
>
> **MACDUFF**
> Approach the chamber, and destroy your sight
> With a new Gorgon. Do not bid me speak;
> See, and then speak yourselves.
>
> *Exeunt MACBETH and LENNOX.*

Starting with this conversation, explore how Shakespeare presents a sense of horror in *Macbeth*.

Write about:

- how Shakespeare presents a sense of horror in this extract

- how Shakespeare presents a sense of horror in the play as a whole.

[30 marks]
AO4 [4 marks]

Zoom in on the question

Starting with this extract, explore how Shakespeare presents a sense of horror in *Macbeth*.

Write about:

- how Shakespeare presents a sense of horror in this extract
- how Shakespeare presents a sense of horror in the play as a whole.

First focus on the extract to 'anchor' the question and explore some details.

This is the question focus. Stay relevant to it. Refer to a sense of horror in the play to help you stay on track. (AO1)

Explore Shakespeare's methods, for example the effects of language choices (AO2) to create a sense of horror.

Start with the extract but clarify/explain details with references to the whole play.

Here are some ideas that could be included in an answer to this question and which cover the Assessment Objectives (AOs):

AO1 The presentation of a world out of control. Events and the presentation of horror used to show the state of chaos in the world and link to Macbeth's mental and moral state.

AO2 How language choices create a sense of horror. Language choices suggesting, for example, an unnatural world – 'lamenting', 'screams' and an unstoppable force at work. Shakespeare's presentation of a sense of chaos.

AO3 How regicide overturns God's will – links to the divine right of kings and body politic.

A student has decided to focus on how different audiences understand the concept of horror. This is the plan they have made to answer the question. Note how the student intends to compare the extract to other parts of the play throughout their answer.

Paragraph	Content		Timing
1	Introduction: use question preparation to establish focus of answer, and my key idea – how different audiences understand the concept of horror.		9.40
2	Explore extract – focus on how Lennox's language creates a sense of unstoppable forces at work and Macduff's shocked reaction.		9.43
3	How Shakespeare establishes a sense of horror through language choices in further examples in play – Macbeth's fearful prediction (Act 1 sc 7) and Macduff's reaction in extract.	Refer to extract and	9.58
4	Nature described as chaos elsewhere in play, for example, Act 3 Sc 2.	question	10.06
5	Role of witches in creating a sense of horror, for example, Act 4 Sc 1.	focus.	10.14
6	Conclusion: brief return to question. How Shakespeare's creation of a sense of horror illustrates a world disrupted by the murder of the King.		10.22

The essay plan above will meet these Assessment Objectives:

AO1 Read, understand and respond	Explore how Shakespeare presents a sense of horror to set the tone of the play and guide the audience's response to Macbeth's actions.
AO2 Language, form and structure	Explore language choices, such as links to chaos and unnatural events in the extract, and how these impact on the tone of the play. Compare with examples elsewhere in the play, for example, the dagger and Banquo's ghost.
AO3 Contexts	Compare audience reactions to events linked to this sense of horror. Shakespeare's reference to body politic and the divine right of kings.

Throughout the play, Shakespeare presents the chaos of Macbeth's world through images resulting in a sense of horror.[1] Many of these images would be familiar to modern audiences used to the horror genre, and contemporary audiences would recognise them from warnings of hell in Christian teachings.

In the extract, Lennox describes the natural world as being in a state of chaos. It is 'unruly', out of control, and the audience senses the horror behind his words as violent weather blows down chimneys with unstoppable force. Shakespeare presents a terrifying cacophony of 'lamentings', suggesting that the natural world is consumed by grief.[2] These cries, joined by 'strange screams', further emphasise their otherworldly nature. These sounds develop by 'prophesying with accents terrible', again reinforcing their difference from the natural world but also reminding the audience of the witches' prophecies that set off this chain of events. Shakespeare presents an **explicit** link between Macbeth and this sense of horror. If the head of state, placed there by God, is murdered – an 'unnatural' deed – the land will face the consequences of this act.[3] These screams are augmented by the sounds of birds that 'clamoured', representing nature's outrage at the chain of horror that Macbeth has unleashed. This is further emphasised by the description of the earth shaking in a 'feverous' state. The sickness metaphor shows the full horror of the corruption inflicted on the world by Duncan's murder as an act against God's will.

This cacophony of sound is silenced by Macbeth's reply,[4] 'Twas a rough night'. As a response to the full horrors of Lennox's description, Macbeth's understatement is almost comical. Through this dramatic irony, Shakespeare makes the audience complicit, as they know what has taken place to make this night 'rough'. The **adjective** 'rough' refers not only to the storm, but to Macbeth's experience: his actions have caused these horrors to be unleashed on the world. This is reinforced by Macduff's simple repetition of 'horror', rendering him inarticulate and providing a sharp contrast to Macbeth's disingenuous response. Here, Shakespeare foreshadows the conflict that will take place between the two men later in the play and reveals their contrasting natures.

Macduff's statement that these horrors can be explained or felt neither by 'Tongue nor heart' links to the fear felt by Macbeth[5] in Act I Scene 7, when he considers during his soliloquy the consequences of killing the 'meek' and 'virtuous' Duncan. Shakespeare presents Macbeth's understanding that by this 'horrid deed' he will face 'damnation'. A contemporary audience will feel the sense of horror underpinning this, as the Church made clear the torments of an eternity in hell as punishment

---

[1] **AO1:** clear opening, using words from the question to ensure relevance.

[2] **AO2 (structure):** clear understanding of how the development of imagery through the play helps Shakespeare to shape meaning and effect.

[3] **AO3:** excellent reference to contemporary beliefs to deepen understanding.

[4] **AO1:** deft choices of details to support points.

[5] **AO2 (structure):** clear understanding of how development of action and imagery through the play help Shakespeare to shape meaning and effect.

for this crime. This understanding is echoed by Macduff's emphatic response, 'O horror, horror, horror'.

This sense of horror presented to show the depravity of Macbeth's actions continues in Act 3. Here the audience sees the impact of this deed on Macbeth's mind, which is 'full of scorpions'.[6] This metaphor, revealing Macbeth's poisoned thoughts, shows his inability to escape this torment. Once again, these scenes take place at night, with evil concealed by darkness. Macbeth's use of images of the occult with 'night's black agents' and its 'yawning peal' reinforces his links to evil and the growing sense of horror.

[6] **AO2:** deft and relevant use of subject terminology.

The play is full of elements found within the horror genre.[7] There are 'daggers' in the air and phantoms with 'gory locks'. In addition, we have the witches presented as breaking down the natural order with their actions. They cause disasters as they 'untie the winds' that 'swallow navigation', a view of witches that would be accepted by a contemporary audience.[8] The horror of acts such as the slaughter of Macduff's wife and children, and the murder of a friend, enable Shakespeare to present a sense of horror in this world where 'unnatural' acts have taken hold.[9]

[7] **AO1/AO3:** clear links to horror and its place in contemporary culture.

[8] **AO3:** clear links to contemporary audience.

[9] **AO2:** insight into Shakespeare's craft as a dramatist.

Shakespeare repeatedly reveals the consequences of the ruthless pursuit of ambition and the horrors that will be unleashed if this 'vaulting ambition' leads to the murder of the king. Shakespeare's creation of a sense of horror clearly illustrates a world disrupted by regicide and serves as a warning to audiences across the centuries.[10]

[10] **AO1/AO3:** clear understanding of key ideas within the play and their relevance to society.

Commentary
This is a thoughtful response that develops a relevant and systematic answer to the question. It is a conceptualised answer based on insights into Shakespeare's presentation of a sense of horror in the play. There are some profound insights based on an appreciation of language details and how Shakespeare structures our responses to the consequences of Macbeth's actions throughout the play.

DO IT!

Now use what you've learned to answer the following AQA exam-style question.

Read the extract from Act 2 Scene 3 of *Macbeth* on page 26.

Starting with this conversation, explore how Shakespeare presents Macbeth's isolation in *Macbeth*.

Write about:

- how Shakespeare presents Macbeth's isolation in this extract
- how Shakespeare presents Macbeth's isolation in the play as a whole.

[30 marks]
AO4 [4 marks]

Read the following extract from Act 2 Scene 4 of *Macbeth* and then answer the question that follows.

At this point in the play, Ross and an Old Man are discussing the strange events that occurred after Duncan's murder.

OLD MAN
Threescore and ten I can remember well,
Within the volume of which time I have seen
Hours dreadful and things strange, but this sore night
Hath trifled former knowings.

ROSS
5   Ah, good father,
Thou seest the heavens, as troubled with man's act,
Threaten his bloody stage. By the clock 'tis day,
And yet dark night strangles the travelling lamp.
Is't night's predominance, or the day's shame,
10 That darkness does the face of earth entomb,
When living light should kiss it?

OLD MAN
'Tis unnatural,
Even like the deed that's done. On Tuesday last
A falcon towering in her pride of place
15 Was by a mousing owl hawk'd at and kill'd.

ROSS
And Duncan's horses – a thing most strange and certain –
Beauteous and swift, the minions of their race,
Turn'd wild in nature, broke their stalls, flung out,
Contending 'gainst obedience, as they would make
20 War with mankind.

OLD MAN
'Tis said they eat each other.

ROSS
They did so, to the amazement of mine eyes
That look'd upon't.

Starting with this extract, explore how Shakespeare presents the natural world in *Macbeth*.

Write about:

- how Shakespeare presents the natural world in this extract

- how Shakespeare presents the natural world in the play as a whole.

[30 marks]
AO4 [4 marks]

Zoom in on the question

Starting with this extract, explore how Shakespeare presents the natural world in *Macbeth*.

Write about:

- how Shakespeare presents the natural world in this extract
- how Shakespeare presents the natural world in the play as a whole.

Concentrate first on the extract, to explore the effects of language choices (AO2) and to clarify the focus of the answer (AO1).

Explore Shakespeare's methods, for example, interpret Shakespeare's ideas about 'natural/unnatural'. (AO2)

Set the extract in the context of the whole play. (AO3)

The topic focus of the question. Establish this focus from the start of the answer. (AO1)

Here are some ideas that could be included in an answer to this question and which cover the Assessment Objectives (AOs):

AO1 The presentation of the natural world in chaos as the result of killing a king (for example, Lennox's speech after Duncan's murder; events depicted in the extract).

AO2 Strong, apocalyptic imagery of nature in chaos to emphasise the breaking down of the natural order: the extract; Lennox's account of a storm the night of Duncan's murder; the witches' ambition to bring chaos to nature, including the weather. Consider how the 'natural order' (for example, justice and the sacred status of kings) is restored at the end of the play.

AO3 Consider the idea of the divine right of kings as context for understanding how nature is presented in the play. Consider the different meanings of 'nature/natural' as used by characters – especially the Macbeths. What are the popular understandings of 'natural' (for example, 'good', 'pure')?

A student has decided to focus on the natural world as the outward sign of 'natural order'. This is the plan they have made to answer the question. Note how the student intends to compare the extract to other parts of the play throughout their answer.

Paragraph	Content		Timing
1	Introduction: use the question prep to establish focus of my answer, and my key idea – natural order, kings, witchcraft.		9.40
2	Explore extract – focus on how language choice reveals meaning.		9.43
3	The idea of 'natural order', kings, evil.	Refer back to extract and question focus throughout. Show consistency of Shakespeare's presentation.	9.58
4	Other examples of chaos in nature as result of unnatural (evil) activity.		10.06
5	Nature and sleep.		10.14
6	Conclusion – brief return to the question. No one can get away with murdering a king: the natural world will give you away.		10.22

The essay plan above will meet these Assessment Objectives:

AO1 Read, understand and respond	Identify the significance of chaos in nature: it is caused by/mirrors evil forces and actions.
AO2 Language, form and structure	Repeated references to natural disaster at personal and environmental levels. Analyse effects of imagery of disaster and confusion in nature.
AO3 Contexts	Setting of analysis in context of contemporary beliefs about kings' holy status.

Throughout *Macbeth* there is a sense of worsening natural disaster, and it is clear that Shakespeare's apocalyptic presentation of the collapsing natural world[1] is linked to treachery, evil and, most importantly, to treason against King and country.[2] When the traitors Macdonwald and the Thane of Cawdor attempt to overthrow their own King, the battle takes place in a thunderstorm, while witches who are 'unnatural' enough to have beards revel in the 'fog and filthy air'. After the 'unnatural' murder of King Duncan, the Macbeths lose the ability to sleep, which is 'nature's second course', and the weather and animals go mad.[3]

This process – evil acts causing an outraged reaction in nature – is very clear in the extract. The Old Man's observation of natural chaos in the wake of Duncan's murder is mild at first: he talks of 'things strange' and 'this sore night', as though there has been only a mild disturbance in nature,[4] but Ross's description goes further and suggests that the killing of a king is going to be fatal for mankind: the day is as dark as night and the darkness 'strangles' the sun and is like a 'tomb'. Ross's morbid imagery reveals his fear that the world is ending.[4] Both characters now compete in their lurid reports of unnatural events: a small owl killed a falcon, and Duncan's horses 'turn'd wild in nature', fighting – and finally eating – each other. This image is ridiculously impossible, but the hyperbole reinforces Ross's 'amazement' and sense of doom.[5]

Their dramatic reports reflect the official view in Shakespeare's time that kings were God-chosen. Killing a king was a crime against God, so after Duncan's murder (probably by his sons which, significantly, Ross later calls "gainst nature'),[6] Ross is not surprised to see nature acting as God's army: it has been so 'troubled with man's acts' that it has declared war on mankind. Both men see chaos in nature as caused by Duncan's murder: the Old Man calls the terrifying, end-of-world weather conditions 'unnatural/Even like the deed [Duncan's murder].'[7] 'Unnatural' is used so often and so automatically by characters as a synonym for evil that kings' divine right to rule is taken for granted: it is natural, not open to question.

Therefore Shakespeare's audience would not have been surprised to hear the murder of a king causes the world to literally fall apart and hurl itself at humans in an 'unruly' way. As Lennox waits for Macduff to collect the king (who is actually dead) he describes the violent storm in the night and how it was full of 'lamentings' and 'screams of death'. In other words, nature was advertising the terrible crime of regicide before it was discovered. Macbeth further links nature and the king when he reports that the stab wounds on Duncan's corpse are 'like a breach in nature'.[8]

1 AO1: clear opening, using words from the question to ensure relevance.

2 AO1: 'conceptual' approach – excellent interpretation of the natural world as a symbol of order/disorder.

3 AO2: deft summary of evidence to support key idea.

4 AO1/AO2: evidence deftly chosen and subtleties of meaning explained.

5 AO2: precise and helpful use of subject terminology, with perceptive comments on effects of specific techniques.

6 AO3: excellent reference to contemporary beliefs to deepen understanding of the role of 'nature' in the play.

7 AO1: perceptive analysis of concept of natural/unnatural and its significance to the action.

8 AO3: Consideration of themes in the extract enriched by comparing their treatment in other parts of the play.

Later, he accuses the evil witches of 'untying the winds' and aiming storms against churches.[8] The Elizabethan idea of order is completed here: the killing of God's representative, the King, has disturbed nature. In turn, this has set free the forces of evil to destroy goodness, symbolised by churches. In this view, the natural order is the social order with the King (and therefore God) at its head.[9]

When the Macbeths sinfully kill Duncan, they too suffer the damage to 'nature' – they can no longer sleep, which is 'nature's second course'. Lady Macbeth tells Macbeth that his mental torment can only be calmed by sleep, which is 'the season of all natures'.[10] She cannot take her own advice though, and by Act 5 she is driven to sleepwalking by what her doctor calls an 'infected mind'.[10] The doctor realises that she has done something that has made the natural world an enemy: he says, 'unnatural deeds breed unnatural troubles.' He suspects that she has committed a sin so great that she can never hope to escape punishment unless she confesses.[11]

The natural world is a source of comfort for humans, but once disturbed by evil it becomes a source of torment, punishment and accusation that will give criminals away. Shakespeare hints at this when Macbeth hesitates to kill Duncan in fear of the natural chaos and storms that would 'blow the horrid deed in every eye.'[12]

[9] **AO1/AO3:** perceptive summing up of the significance of the theme, especially to contemporary audiences.

[10] **AO1:** Deft choices of relevant references to the text.

[11] **AO1:** here the insight into the relationship between nature, sin and order is reinforced.

[12] **AO2:** sensitive appreciation of both literal and metaphoric meaning in Shakespeare's choice of image.

Commentary

This is a profound and exploratory response that develops a relevant and well-structured analysis. It explores a number of original lines of enquiry that are helpfully related to a sharp understanding of the Elizabethan concept of natural order. Textual references, both direct and indirect, are well chosen and deftly analysed in terms of their meaning and effect. Subject terminology is used accurately and usefully to support insights into Shakespeare's intentions.

DO IT!

Now use what you've learned to answer the following AQA exam-style question.

Read the extract from Act 2 Scene 4 of *Macbeth* on page 30.

Starting with this extract, explore how Shakespeare presents feelings of horror or fear in *Macbeth*.

Write about:

- how Shakespeare presents feelings of horror or fear at this moment in the play
- how Shakespeare presents feelings of horror or fear in the play as a whole.

[30 marks]
AO4 [4 marks]

Read the following extract from Act 1 Scene 7 of *Macbeth* and then answer the question that follows.

As the Macbeths plan to murder Duncan, Macbeth worries about the consequences of killing him. Lady Macbeth is appalled by his change of mind.

LADY MACBETH
What cannot you and I perform upon
The unguarded Duncan? What not put upon
His spongy officers, who shall bear the guilt
Of our great quell?

MACBETH
5   Bring forth men-children only,
For thy undaunted mettle should compose
Nothing but males. Will it not be received,
When we have mark'd with blood those sleepy two
Of his own chamber and used their very daggers,
10   That they have done't?

LADY MACBETH
Who dares receive it other,
As we shall make our griefs and clamour roar
Upon his death?

MACBETH
I am settled, and bend up
15   Each corporal agent to this terrible feat.
Away, and mock the time with fairest show:
False face must hide what the false heart doth know.

Starting with this conversation, explore how Shakespeare presents the relationship between Macbeth and Lady Macbeth in *Macbeth*.

Write about:

- how Shakespeare presents the relationship between Macbeth and Lady Macbeth in this extract

- how Shakespeare presents the relationship between Macbeth and Lady Macbeth in the play as a whole.

[30 marks]
AO4 [4 marks]

Zoom in on the question

First focus on the extract to 'anchor' the question and explore some details.

Starting with this conversation, explore how Shakespeare presents the relationship between Macbeth and Lady Macbeth in *Macbeth*.

Write about:

- how Shakespeare presents the relationship between Macbeth and Lady Macbeth in this extract

- how Shakespeare presents the relationship between Macbeth and Lady Macbeth in the play as a whole.

Explore Shakespeare's methods, for example, the effects of language choices (AO2) to reveal their relationship.

This is the question focus. Stay relevant to it. Refer to their relationship and how it develops in the play to help you stay on track. (AO1/2)

Start with the extract but clarify/explain details with references to the whole play.

Here are some ideas that could be included in an answer to this question and which cover the Assessment Objectives (AOs):

AO1 Presentation of a relationship that is constantly changing. Elements of power and how the power balance shifts during the play. Events that spotlight the shifting nature of their relationship. Theme of appearance and reality – how assuming roles destroys the relationship.

AO2 How language choices allow the audience to see the inner workings of their relationship. Language choices suggesting tenderness/scorn/dismissal. Presentation of power within the relationship.

AO3 Use of modern audience to contextualise the relationship. Position of women in 17th century. Development of the relationship within the context of the play's structure.

A student has decided to focus on the development of Macbeth and Lady Macbeth's relationship throughout the play. This is the plan they have made to answer the question. Note how the student intends to compare the extract to other parts of the play throughout their answer.

Paragraph	Content		Timing
1	Introduction: use question preparation to establish focus of answer, and my key idea – how Shakespeare presents the changing power dynamic between M and Lady M.		9.40
2	Exploration of a modern audience's view of the relationship. The relationship at the start of the play as a modern equal partnership.		9.43
3	Focus on extract and shift in power as M returns to the castle. Lady M as ruthless 'fiend-like queen' within the relationship.	Refer back to extract and question focus.	9.58
4	Shift in the dynamic as M independently orders the murder of Banquo. Lady M's role to soothe Lords at banquet and scold M.		10.06
5	Further shift in the dynamic at the end of the play. Macbeth's distance and Lady Macbeth's madness and death.		10.14
6	Conclusion – brief return to question. How Shakespeare presents a relationship in decline.		10.22

The essay plan above will meet these Assessment Objectives:

AO1 Read, understand and respond	Explore how Shakespeare uses this relationship to set the tone of the play and guide the audience's response to Macbeth's actions.
AO2 Language, form and structure	Explore language choices in the extract, and how these might impact on the tone of the play. Compare with examples elsewhere in the play.
AO3 Contexts	Comment on likely reactions of a modern audience. Development of the relationship within the context of the play's structure, for example, how it changes and declines as the play progresses.

The relationship between Lady Macbeth and Macbeth can be viewed as a relationship high in affection and ambition at the start of the play.[1] Sadly, by the end of the play this relationship has descended into failure. Modern theatre and film directors have enjoyed exploring this dynamic between the couple.[2]

Audiences today will view this marriage as a modern relationship, with the couple as equal partners.[3] Macbeth shares his meeting with the witches while referring to her as his 'dearest', an affectionate term. In contrast, Lady MacDuff complains to Ross that MacDuff has abandoned the family, as he does not share details of his flight to England, stating 'He loves us not'. Lady Macbeth, however, understands her husband and his motivations, showing their close relationship. She fears he is 'too full o' the milk of human kindness' and he does not have the 'illness' that ambition requires. This sickness[4] image suggests that ambition is a corrupting force and it is ironic that she misjudges her husband's capacity for such ambition, for it is this ambition that causes his downfall. Lady Macbeth knows the power she wields over her husband and embraces it, claiming she will 'chastise' with the 'valour of my tongue to change his mind'.

Lady Macbeth's power over Macbeth is revealed when Macbeth returns to the castle. The audience has seen her use direct, shocking language when she calls on the 'spirits' to 'take my milk for gall' as she seeks to purge the nourishing essence of womanhood and make it poison.[5] The brutality of her language is revealed through her monosyllabic words, 'and pall thee', linking this funeral image to the 'smoke of hell'. In the extract we see how she can assume the role of persuader as she seductively sells her ideas through repeated rhetorical questions: 'What cannot you and I perform?', tempting him through her inclusive language.[6] In response, Macbeth recognises her determination, praising her 'undaunted mettle' and her ambition and ruthlessness. Here the audience sees them as partners, as Lady Macbeth considers that they will be able to point the blame for the murder elsewhere. Finally Macbeth is 'settled' and decisive, asserting that, 'False face must hide what false heart must know'. This image of a mask of truth signals the beginning of the disintegration of their marriage.[7] The audience recognises that a relationship containing pretence and deception will fail.

By Act 3 Scene I we begin to see cracks in their partnership. Macbeth does not include Lady Macbeth in his plans to kill Banquo and Fleance, revealing a shift in the balance of power. We also see Lady Macbeth seeking to control the opinions of the Lords as well as control Macbeth's

1 AO1: clear opening, using words from the question to ensure relevance.

2 AO1/AO3: 'conceptual' approach – question focus viewed from POV of modern audience.

3 AO3: excellent reference to contemporary beliefs to deepen understanding.

4 AO2 (structure): clear understanding of how development of imagery through the play helps Shakespeare to shape meaning and effect.

5 AO2: clear understanding of imagery through the play to shape meaning and effect.

6 AO1: deft choices of details to support points.

7 AO1/AO3: clear understanding of the development of Macbeth and Lady Macbeth's relationship and the impact on the audience.

reactions to Banquo's ghost in Act 3 scene 4. Instead of manipulation and persuasion,[8] Lady Macbeth pours scorn on Macbeth: 'O proper stuff!', the exclamation reminding him that this is 'Shame itself'. Yet, however powerful her words may seem with her allusion to dishonour and disgrace, she has lost control of her husband, as Macbeth no longer needs her support in his quest for power.

Lady Macbeth's guilt and torment, presented through her 'infected mind', show the depth of the decline of their marriage at the end of the play. When Macbeth asks the doctor to cure her 'diseased' mind, the unexpected tenderness surprises an audience already accustomed to their distance.[9] However, this tenderness does not last. When told his wife is dead his response is stoic. He has reached a state where life signifies 'nothing' and his love for his 'dearest partner in greatness' has been swept aside in readiness to face Macduff.

As Lady Macbeth and Macbeth assume different roles[10] to gain power by taking on 'false faces' in order to hide their true desires, so the balance of power in their relationship causes their relationship to fail.

[8] **AO2**: deft and relevant use of subject terminology.

[9] **AO2**: insight into Shakespeare's craft as a dramatist.

AO1: clear return to question focus to conclude the response.

Commentary
This is a thoughtful response that develops a relevant and systematic answer to the question. This is a conceptualised answer based on insights into Shakespeare's presentation of the relationship between Macbeth and Lady Macbeth. There are some profound ideas based on an appreciation of language details and how Shakespeare structures our responses to the consequences of Macbeth's actions throughout the play and their impact on this central relationship.

DO IT!

Read the extract from Act 1 Scene 7 of *Macbeth* on page 34.

Starting with this conversation, explore how Shakespeare presents ideas about truth and lies in *Macbeth*.

Write about:

• how Shakespeare presents ideas about truth and lies in this extract

• how Shakespeare presents ideas about truth and lies in the play as a whole.

[30 marks]
AO4 [4 marks]

Read the following extract from Act 5 Scene 1 of *Macbeth* and then answer the question that follows.

At this point in the play, Lady Macbeth's servant, a Gentlewoman, has asked a doctor to observe Lady Macbeth as she sleepwalks.

DOCTOR
What a sigh is there! The heart is sorely charged.

GENTLEWOMAN
I would not have such a heart in my bosom for the dignity of the whole body.

DOCTOR
Well, well, well –

GENTLEWOMAN
Pray God it be, sir.

DOCTOR
5   This disease is beyond my practice. Yet I have known those which have walked in
their sleep who have died holily in their beds.

LADY MACBETH
Wash your hands, put on your nightgown, look not so pale. I tell you yet again,
Banquo's buried; he cannot come out on's grave.

DOCTOR
Even so?

LADY MACBETH
10   To bed, to bed; there's knocking at the gate. Come,
come, come, come, give me your hand. What's done cannot be undone.
To bed, to bed, to bed. [*Exit.*]

DOCTOR
Will she go now to bed?

GENTLEWOMAN
Directly.

DOCTOR
15   Foul whisperings are abroad. Unnatural deeds
Do breed unnatural troubles; infected minds
To their deaf pillows will discharge their secrets.

Starting with this moment in the play, explore how Shakespeare presents mental torment in *Macbeth*.

Write about:

- how Shakespeare presents mental torment in this discussion about Lady Macbeth's state of mind

- how Shakespeare presents mental torment in the play as a whole.

[30 marks]
AO4 [4 marks]

Read the following extract from Act 3 Scene 1 of *Macbeth* and then answer the question that follows.

At this point in the play, Macbeth has spoken with Banquo and learned that he is about to go riding with his son Fleance.

MACBETH
To be thus is nothing,
But to be safely thus. Our fears in Banquo
Stick deep, and in his royalty of nature
Reigns that which would be fear'd. 'Tis much he dares,
5   And, to that dauntless temper of his mind,
He hath a wisdom that doth guide his valour
To act in safety. There is none but he
Whose being I do fear; and under him
My genius is rebuked, as it is said
10   Mark Antony's was by Caesar. He chid the sisters
When first they put the name of King upon me
And bade them speak to him; then prophet-like
They hail'd him father to a line of kings.
Upon my head they placed a fruitless crown
15   And put a barren sceptre in my gripe,
Thence to be wrench'd with an unlineal hand,
No son of mine succeeding. If't be so,
For Banquo's issue have I filed my mind,
For them the gracious Duncan have I murder'd,
20   Put rancours in the vessel of my peace
Only for them, and mine eternal jewel
Given to the common enemy of man,
To make them kings – the seed of Banquo kings!
Rather than so, come, Fate, into the list,
25   And champion me to the utterance!

Starting with this moment in the play, explore how Shakespeare presents Banquo in *Macbeth*.

Write about:

- how Shakespeare presents the character of Banquo in this extract

- how Shakespeare presents Banquo in the play as a whole.

[30 marks]
AO4 [4 marks]

Read the following extract from Act 3 Scene 4 of *Macbeth* and then answer the question that follows.

At this point in the play, Lady Macbeth tries to calm Macbeth after he has seen Banquo's ghost at their feast.

LADY MACBETH
O proper stuff!
This is the very painting of your fear;
This is the air-drawn dagger which you said
Led you to Duncan. O, these flaws and starts,
5   Impostors to true fear, would well become
A woman's story at a winter's fire,
Authorized by her grandam. Shame itself!
Why do you make such faces? When all's done,
You look but on a stool.

MACBETH
10   Prithee, see there! Behold! Look! Lo! How say you?
Why, what care I? If thou canst nod, speak too.
If charnel houses and our graves must send
Those that we bury back, our monuments
Shall be the maws of kites.

Exit GHOST.

LADY MACBETH
15   What, quite unmann'd in folly?

MACBETH
If I stand here, I saw him.

LADY MACBETH
Fie, for shame!

MACBETH
Blood hath been shed ere now, i' the olden time;
Ere humane statute purged the gentle weal;
20   Ay, and since too, murders have been perform'd
Too terrible for the ear. The time has been,
That, when the brains were out, the man would die,
And there an end; but now they rise again,
With twenty mortal murders on their crowns,
25   And push us from our stools. This is more strange
Than such a murder is.

Starting with this conversation, explore how Shakespeare presents visions or imagination in *Macbeth*.

Write about:

- how Shakespeare presents visions or imagination in this extract

- how Shakespeare presents visions or imagination in the play as a whole.

[30 marks]
AO4 [4 marks]

Read the following extract from Act 5 Scene 1 of *Macbeth* and then answer the question that follows.

At this point in the play, Lady Macbeth, watched by her servant and a doctor, sleepwalks in a state of anxiety.

LADY MACBETH
Out, damned spot! Out, I say! One – two – why then 'tis time to do't. Hell is murky. Fie, my lord, fie! A soldier, and afeard? What need we fear who knows it, when none can call our power to account? Yet who would have thought the
5   old man to have had so much blood in him?

DOCTOR
Do you mark that?

LADY MACBETH
The Thane of Fife had a wife; where is she now? What, will these hands ne'er be clean? No more o' that, my lord, no more o' that. You mar all with this starting.

DOCTOR
10   Go to, go to; you have known what you should not.

GENTLEWOMAN
She has spoke what she should not, I am sure of that. Heaven knows what she has known.

LADY MACBETH
Here's the smell of the blood still. All the perfumes of Arabia will not sweeten this little hand. Oh, oh, oh!

DOCTOR
15   What a sigh is there! The heart is sorely charged.

GENTLEWOMAN
I would not have such a heart in my bosom for the dignity of the whole body.

Starting with this moment in the play, explore how Shakespeare presents ideas about guilt in *Macbeth*.

Write about:

• how Shakespeare presents ideas about guilt in this extract

• how Shakespeare presents ideas about guilt in the play as a whole.

[30 marks]
AO4 [4 marks]

Read the following extract from Act 1 Scene 5 of *Macbeth* and then answer the question that follows.

At this point in the play, Lady Macbeth welcomes Macbeth home from battle.

Lady Macbeth
                    Come, thick night,
And pall thee in the dunnest smoke of hell
That my keen knife see not the wound it makes
Nor heaven peep through the blanket of the dark,
5   To cry, 'Hold, hold!'

Enter MACBETH.

Great Glamis! Worthy Cawdor!
Greater than, both by the all-hail hereafter!

…

Macbeth
My dearest love,
Duncan comes here tonight.

Lady Macbeth
10   And when goes hence?

Macbeth
Tomorrow, as he purposes.

Lady Macbeth
O, never
Shall sun that morrow see!
Your face, my Thane, is as a book where men
15   May read strange matters. To beguile the time,
Look like the time; bear welcome in your eye,
Your hand, your tongue; look like the innocent flower,
But be the serpent under it. He that's coming
Must be provided for; and you shall put
20   This night's great business into my dispatch,
Which shall to all our nights and days to come
Give solely sovereign sway and masterdom.

Macbeth
We will speak further.

Lady Macbeth
Only look up clear;
25   To alter favour ever is to fear.

Starting with this moment in the play, explore how Shakespeare presents ideas about deception in *Macbeth*.

Write about:

- how Shakespeare presents ideas about deception in this extract

- how Shakespeare presents ideas about deception in the play as a whole.

[30 marks]
AO4 [4 marks]

Read the following extract from Act 1 Scene 7 of *Macbeth* and then answer the question that follows.

At this point in the play, Macbeth considers whether he should kill Duncan.

Macbeth

    If it were done when 'tis done, then 'twere well
    It were done quickly. If the assassination
    Could trammel up the consequence, and catch,
    With his surcease, success; that but this blow
5   Might be the be-all and the end-all – here,
    But here, upon this bank and shoal of time,
    We'd jump the life to come. But in these cases
    We still have judgment here, that we but teach
    Bloody instructions, which being taught return
10   To plague the inventor. This even-handed justice
    Commends the ingredients of our poison'd chalice
    To our own lips. He's here in double trust:
    First, as I am his kinsman and his subject,
    Strong both against the deed; then, as his host,
15   Who should against his murderer shut the door,
    Not bear the knife myself. Besides, this Duncan
    Hath borne his faculties so meek, hath been
    So clear in his great office, that his virtues
    Will plead like angels trumpet-tongued against
20   The deep damnation of his taking-off,
    And pity, like a naked new-born babe
    Striding the blast, or heaven's cherubim horsed
    Upon the sightless couriers of the air,
    Shall blow the horrid deed in every eye,
25   That tears shall drown the wind. I have no spur
    To prick the sides of my intent, but only
    Vaulting ambition, which o'erleaps itself
    And falls on the other.

Starting with this moment in the play, explore how Shakespeare presents the theme of ambition in *Macbeth*.

Write about:

*   how Shakespeare presents Macbeth's ambition in this extract

*   how Shakespeare presents ambition in the play as a whole.

[30 marks]
AO4 [4 marks]

Read the following extract from Act 1 Scene 4 of *Macbeth* and then answer the question that follows.

At this point in the play, Duncan welcomes Macbeth and Banquo on their victorious return from battle.

MACBETH
The service and the loyalty I owe,
In doing it, pays itself. Your Highness' part
Is to receive our duties, and our duties
Are to your throne and state, children and servants,
5   Which do but what they should, by doing everything
Safe toward your love and honour.

DUNCAN
Welcome hither.
I have begun to plant thee, and will labour
To make thee full of growing. Noble Banquo,
10 That hast no less deserved, nor must be known
No less to have done so; let me enfold thee
And hold thee to my heart.

BANQUO
There if I grow,
The harvest is your own.

DUNCAN
15 My plenteous joys,
Wanton in fullness, seek to hide themselves
In drops of sorrow. Sons, kinsmen, thanes,
And you whose places are the nearest, know
We will establish our estate upon
20 Our eldest, Malcolm, whom we name hereafter
The Prince of Cumberland; which honour must
Not unaccompanied invest him only,
But signs of nobleness, like stars, shall shine
On all deservers. From hence to Inverness,
25 And bind us further to you.

Starting with this extract, explore how Shakespeare presents the relationship between kings and their subjects.

Write about:

- how Shakespeare presents the relationship between kings and their subjects at this moment in the play

- how Shakespeare presents the relationship between kings and their subjects in the play as a whole.

[30 marks]
AO4 [4 marks]

Read the following extract from Act 4 Scene 2 of *Macbeth* and then answer the question that follows.

At this point in the play, Ross and Lady Macduff discuss Macduff's journey to England, leaving his family and castle undefended.

LADY MACDUFF
Wisdom? To leave his wife, to leave his babes,
His mansion and his titles, in a place
From whence himself does fly? He loves us not;
He wants the natural touch; for the poor wren,
5   The most diminutive of birds, will fight,
Her young ones in her nest, against the owl.
All is the fear and nothing is the love;
As little is the wisdom, where the flight
So runs against all reason.

ROSS
10   My dearest coz,
I pray you, school yourself. But for your husband,
He is noble, wise, judicious, and best knows
The fits o' the season. I dare not speak much further;
But cruel are the times when we are traitors
15   And do not know ourselves; when we hold rumour
From what we fear, yet know not what we fear,
But float upon a wild and violent sea
Each way and move. I take my leave of you;
Shall not be long but I'll be here again.
20   Things at the worst will cease or else climb upward
To what they were before. My pretty cousin,
Blessing upon you!

Starting with this moment in the play, explore how Shakespeare presents Macduff in *Macbeth*.

Write about:

- how Shakespeare presents the character of Macduff in this extract
- how Shakespeare presents Macduff in the play as a whole.

[30 marks]
AO4 [4 marks]

Glossary

adjective A word that describes a noun (for example: d*readful* note; *restless* ecstasy).

blank verse Poetry that does not rhyme.

character A person in a play or story: a person created by the writer (for example: Macbeth, Lady Macbeth or Banquo).

connotation An implied meaning. See **implicit.**

context The circumstances in which a play was written or is watched. These could include normal beliefs at the turn of the 17th century, or the typical attitudes of a 21st-century audience.

dramatic irony When the audience knows more than a character (for example, at the beginning of Act 1 Scene 6, when Duncan and Banquo feel safe and relaxed but the audience knows that Duncan is far from safe).

dramatist Playwright: the author of a play.

effect The impact that a writer's words have on a reader: the mood, feeling or reaction the words create in the reader/viewer.

explicit Explicit information is clearly stated; it's on the surface of a text and should be obvious.

extract Part of a text. AQA will choose an extract from Macbeth as a starting point for your exam answer.

Greek chorus Ancient Greek drama normally included a 'chorus' – a group of unnamed characters who would comment on the action of the play, guiding the audience's reactions.

hyperbole Exaggerated statements or claims not meant to be taken literally. Used for rhetorical effect.

imagery The 'pictures' an author puts into the reader's mind. Similes and metaphors are common types of imagery. Macbeth is full of imagery linked to clothes, darkness, night.

interpret (interpretation) Use clues to work out meanings or the feelings or motives of a character.

language The words and the style that a writer *chooses* in order to have an effect on a reader.

melodramatic Extremely or very emotionally dramatic, almost to the point of being unbelievable.

metaphor Comparing two things by referring to them as though they are the same thing (for example, Macbeth says his mind is *'full of scorpions'*. It is not *literally* full of scorpions.).

monosyllable A word with just one syllable (for example: *Ross, thane, my*).

phrase A group of words within a sentence.

playwright The author of a play.

plot The story of the play: the sequence of the events and how they link together.

rhetoric Words used for persuasive effect.

rhetorical question A question that does not need an answer. Normally used for persuasive purposes.

rhyme Words chosen by a poet because they have the same sound (for example: *he/flea; stable/label; laughter/after*).

rhyming couplet Two consecutive lines that rhyme.

rhythm The beat in poetry or music.

structure How a text is organised and held together: all those things that shape a text and make it coherent. For example, Macbeth is arranged into five acts; it follows the sequence of a traditional 'tragedy'; it has repeated patterns of imagery of the supernatural.

subject terminology The technical words that are used in a particular subject. All the words in this glossary are subject terminology for English literature.

tone The mood of a text, or the attitude of the author or narrator towards the topic. For example, tones can be mocking, affectionate, polite, authoritative.

trochaic meter The reverse of an iambic meter: trochaic meter alternates between first a stressed syllable and then an unstressed one.

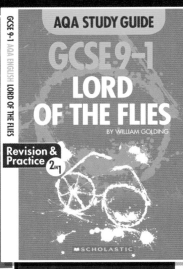
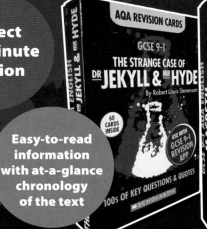

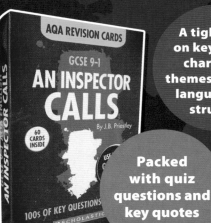
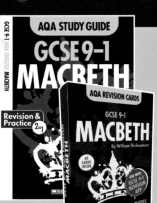
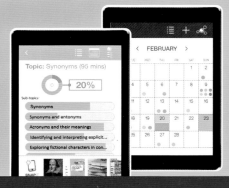